Basketball game newbie coaches and players

Rules, fouls, violations, dribbling in basketball game

Carl Michaels

Copyright ©2023 by Carl Michaels. All rights are reserved. Without prior permission from Amazon KDP, no portion of this book may be duplicated or transmitted in any way, whether it be electronically or mechanically, including by photocopying, recording, or information storage and retrieval systems.

TABLE OF CONTENTS

INTRODUCTION

CHAPTER ONE   An overview of a basketball game: its growth and popularity

CHAPTER TWO Equipment and playing field

CHAPTER THREE Number of players, positions in a team, team roster, and game officials

CHAPTER FOUR   The objective of the game; Scoring points and Winning the game

CHAPTER FIVE Fouls in the basketball game

CHAPTER SIX Violations in Basketball and Time Regulations

CHAPTER SEVEN Dribbling the Basketball

CHAPTER EIGHT Shooting the ball, rules of substitution, and the greatest players

INTRODUCTION

A fast-paced, thrilling sport that is played by millions of people worldwide, that is,
basketball. Basketball is a fantastic sport for staying healthy, developing cooperation skills, and having fun, whether you play competitively or just with your friends. But understanding the game's regulations is crucial if you want to enjoy basketball to its fullest. Every part of the game, from dribbling and passing to shooting and rebounding, has precise regulations that must be observed to ensure fair play and a fun experience for everyone.

Basketball is a game that many people around the world are quite enthusiastic about. The game was invented by James Naismith in 1891, and it has since developed into one of the most well-liked sports in the world. Basketball is a sport in which two teams of five players each attempt to earn points by putting the ball through the net of the opposing team's basket. Basketball rules comprehension is essential for good play. Dribbling, passing, shooting, and rebounding are all covered by these rules. Players are subject to restrictions on movement and interactivity with other players.

The shot clock, which guarantees that both sides have an equal opportunity to score, is one of basketball's most crucial rules. The shot clock limits the amount of time each team has to take a shot before the ball is passed to the opposition. The traveling violation, which happens when a player moves the ball while not dribbling, takes too many steps or shifts their pivot foot, is another important basketball rule. Such violations may lead to a turnover or a loss of possession.

In general, basketball regulations encourage fair play and a fun experience for all players and spectators. Both players and spectators must be aware of these regulations to advance their abilities and enjoy the game to its fullest. We will examine the fundamentals of the basketball game and its rules in this article, giving readers a basis for learning more about this well-liked sport.

CHAPTER ONE

An overview of a basketball game: its growth and popularity

To keep his gym class active in the early days of December 1891, Canadian-American Dr. James Naismith, a physical education professor at the International Young Men's Christian Association Training School (YMCA), which is now Springfield College, in Springfield, Massachusetts, created the game of basketball. He looked for a challenging indoor game to keep his kids engaged and in good physical shape through the long New England winters. In response to his rejection of alternative concepts as being either too rough or unsuitable for walled-in gymnasiums, the basic rules were written and a peach basket was added to a 10-foot (3.05 m) raised track. When a "basket" or point was scored, the balls in this peach basket had to be manually gathered, in contrast to modern basketball nets that have detachable bottoms. The bottom of the basket was removed after this proved ineffectual.

Initially, basketball was played with a soccer ball. The orange ball that is currently in use was only developed by Tony Hinkle in the late 1950s. Brown was the color of the first basketballs designed specifically for basketball. Dribbling was absent from the original game, save for the "bounce pass" to teammates. Passing was the primary way to move the ball. Early balls were asymmetrical, which limited the spread of dribbling.

Once manufacturers altered the shape of the ball, dribbling was introduced in the 1950s. Peach baskets were still in use up until 1906. Metal hoops with backboards were adopted the year after that. Another modification was made and the ball simply went through. Each time a player placed the ball in the goal, his team would receive a point. After the match, the side with the most points triumphed. The initial placement of the baskets on the mezzanine balcony of the playing court became untenable when spectators began blocking shots. The backboard was created to prevent this interference in addition to facilitating rebound shots.

The new sport was given the name "Basketball" by Naismith. Nine players took part in the first-ever official game, which was played on January 20, 1892, in the YMCA gym in Albany, New York. The shot was made from 25 feet (7.6 m) and the game concluded with a 1-0 score on a court that was only half the size of a contemporary Streetball or National Basketball Association (NBA) floor. By 1897–1898, five-person teams were the rule.

College Basketball

Early backers were given to YMCAs all around the country, and basketball quickly gained popularity in the USA and Canada. It had firmly taken root by 1895 in a large number of women's high schools. The YMCA was in charge of the game's early development and popularization, but after ten years it started to oppose the new sport as harsh play and rowdy spectators started to interfere with the YMCA's main goals. Nonetheless, the position was quickly filled by other collegiate and professional organizations, amateur sports leagues, and universities. The Amateur Athletic Union and the Intercollegiate Athletic Association of the United States (the NCAA's predecessor) fought over control of the rules of the game at the onset of World War I. To safeguard players from exploitation and encourage a less brutal game, the National Basketball League, the first professional league, was established in 1898.

Dr. James Naismith contributed to collegiate basketball's development. The first basketball squad for collegiate players was founded by his colleague C.O. Beamis just one year after the Springfield YMCA game at Geneva College in Pittsburgh. Finally, Naismith served as the University of Kansas' head coach for six years before handing the reins to legendary coach Forrest "Phog" Allen. Adolph Rupp, a follower of Naismith who attended the University of Kentucky, had considerable success as a coach there, while Amos Alonzo Stagg, a follower of Naismith who attended Kansas, introduced basketball to the University of Chicago. The first intercollegiate 5-on-5 game was played on February 9, 1895, between Hamline University and the School of Agriculture, a division of the University of Minnesota. The final score was 9-3 in favor of the School of Agriculture.

Several universities started sponsoring men's athletics in 1901, including Yale University, the University of Chicago, Columbia University, Dartmouth College, the University of Minnesota, the U.S. Naval Academy, and the University of Colorado. Due to the increasing number of accidents on football fields, President Theodore Roosevelt suggested that universities establish a governing organization. As a result, the Intercollegiate Athletic Association of the United States was founded in 1905. (IAAUS). The National Collegiate Athletic Association became the name of the organization in 1910. (NCAA). The first intercollegiate basketball game in Canada was played on February 6, 1904, when McGill University traveled to Queen's University. The game was held in the Kingston, Ontario, YMCA. When regulation play concluded with a score of 7, the match's winner was decided after a ten-minute overtime period (9-7 for McGill).

The first men's national championship competition, the National Association of Intercollegiate Athletics (NAIA) championship, which is now known as the National Association of Intercollegiate Basketball tournament, was established in 1937. Both the inspiration for the NCAA's national tournament and the first occasion for an NCAA team to win a national title were provided by the National Invitation Tournament (NIT), which was founded in 1938 in New York. The NIT lost support to the NCAA tournament due to a history of cheating.

High school basketball

Before large school district mergers, the vast majority of high schools in America were much smaller than they are today. Due to its cheap resource and labor demands, basketball swiftly gained popularity as the ideal interscholastic sport in the first half of the 20th century. Basketball was hugely popular during high school in most of America before college and professional sports received a lot of media attention. The greatest high school basketball team in history may be the Franklin Miracle Five from Indiana, who dominated Indiana basketball in the 1920s and received widespread praise.

On days when the calendar is even, basketball varsity games are played between teams from nearly all American high schools. Basketball is still a sport that many people still regard, especially in rural areas where it acts as a unifying symbol for the entire community and at some renowned institutions with illustrious basketball programs where many players continue to play at higher levels after graduation. The National Federation of State High School Associations reports that during the 2003–2004 academic year, 1,002,797 boys and girls competed for their schools in interscholastic basketball. In Illinois, Indiana, and Kentucky, high school basketball, or Hoosier Hysteria as it is called there, is wildly popular. The significance of high school basketball to these communities is highlighted in the well-known film Hoosiers.

From 1917 through 1930, the National Interscholastic Basketball Tournament served as the University of Chicago's main competition. The competition was organized by Amos Alonzo Stagg, who also invited participants from the winning states. The event has grown since it first started as a tournament for the Midwest region. In 1929, 29 state champions made up the field of competitors.

Loyola University hosted the National Catholic Interscholastic Basketball Tournament from 1924 through 1941. Catholic University, Georgetown, and George Mason were a few of the venues where the National Catholic Invitational Basketball Tournament was contested between 1954 and 1978. From 1929 until 1942, Hampton Institute served as the venue for the National Interscholastic Basketball Tournament for Black High Schools. The National Invitational Interscholastic Basketball Tournament was conducted at Tuskegee Institute from 1941 through 1967. It was resumed at Tennessee State College in Nashville after being put on hold during World War II. After Brown v. Board of Education, which resulted in school desegregation in 1954, the champion's prestige started to decline. In 1964 and 1967, the competitions were conducted at Alabama State College.

Professional basketball

Throughout the 1920s, teams were everywhere. In towns and cities around the country, there were countless men's professional basketball teams, but the league was not well organized. Teams competed in armories and smokey dance halls while players switched between them. Leagues were in and out. Barnstorming teams like the Original Celtics and two all-African American teams, the New York Renaissance Five ("Rens") and the (still active) Harlem Globetrotters, competed in up to 200 games annually while on national tours.

The American Basketball Association (BAA) was established in 1946. On November 1, 1946, the Toronto Huskies and the New York Knickerbockers played their debut game in Toronto, Ontario, Canada. The BAA and National Basketball League combined three years later, in 1949, to establish the National Basketball Association (NBA). A rise in interest in professional basketball was made possible by the 1950s when basketball had established itself as a significant collegiate sport. In Springfield, Massachusetts, the location of the inaugural game, a basketball hall of fame was established in 1959. Its rosters feature the names of outstanding players, coaches, officials, and other individuals who have made important contributions to the growth of the game. Those who have achieved a lot in their basketball careers are members of the hall of fame. Before the ABA and NBA united in 1976, a fledgling group known as the American Basketball Association briefly threatened the NBA's hegemony. In terms of fandom, earnings, talent, and degree of competitiveness, the NBA is currently the best professional basketball league in the world. The NBA established the NBDL, a developmental league, in 2001. In 2012, there were 16 clubs in the league.

International basketball

Eight founding countries—Argentina, Czechoslovakia, Greece, Italy, Latvia, Portugal, Romania, and Switzerland—formed the International Basketball Federation in 1932. The group was only in charge of amateur players at the time. "FIBA" was its abbreviation, which stood for Fédération Internationale de Basketball Amateur in French. Although a trial event was held in 1904, men's basketball was first featured at the Berlin Summer Olympics in 1936. In the inaugural outdoor final, the United States defeated Canada. The United States has often dominated this competition; their team has won all but three championships, with the first defeat coming in a contentious final match against the Soviet Union in Munich in 1972. The first men's FIBA World Championship took place in Argentina in 1950. The first FIBA World Championship for Women took place in Chile three years later. In 1976, when the Olympics were being held in Montreal, Canada, women's basketball was added to the program. Teams from the Soviet Union, Brazil, and Australia competed against the American teams.

In 1989, FIBA abolished the distinction between amateur and professional players, and in 1992, professional players participated in Olympic competitions for the first time. With the debut of their Dream Team, the United States maintained its domination. Yet when other nations' programs advanced, they began to defeat the US national teams. At the 2002 World Championships in Indianapolis, a team made up entirely of NBA players placed sixth, trailing only Yugoslavia, Argentina, Germany, New Zealand, and Spain. The United States suffered its first Olympic defeat while fielding professional athletes in the 2004 Athens Olympics, losing to Puerto Rico (by a score of 19 points) and Lithuania in group play before losing to Argentina in the quarterfinals. After overcoming Lithuania, it came in third place, behind Argentina and Italy. The United States reached the semifinals of the World Championship of Japan in 2006 but lost to Greece by a score of 101-95. It defeated team Argentina in the bronze medal match and came in third place, just behind Greece and Spain. After the failures of 2002 through 2006, the United States got back together and reclaimed its position as the world's best team, surpassing the "Redeem Team," which won the 2008 Olympics, and the so-called "B-Team," which won the 2010 FIBA World Championship in Turkey despite not having any members of the 2008 squad.

The all-tournament teams from the FIBA World Championships in 2002 and 2006, which were hosted in Indianapolis and Japan, respectively, reflect the game's tremendous globalization. In 2006, Carmelo Anthony was the lone American on either team. Nowitzki, Ginobili, Yao, Peja Stojakovic of Yugoslavia (now of Serbia), and Pero Cameron of New Zealand made up the 2002 squad. The 2006 team also included Ginobili, along with Anthony, Gasol, Jorge Garbajosa from Spain, and Theodoros Papaloukas from Greece. Cameron and Papaloukas are the only players on each squad who have never played in the NBA. MVP Kevin Durant of Team USA and the Oklahoma City Thunder, Linas Kleiza of Lithuania and the Toronto Raptors, Luis Scola of Argentina and the Houston Rockets, and Hedo Türkolu of Turkey and the Phoenix Suns all made the all-tournament team from the 2010 edition in Turkey. Serbian Milo Teodosi was the lone non-NBA player. The fact that Team USA failed to win any of the three world championships contested between 1998 and 2006, with Serbia (formerly known as Yugoslavia) triumphing in 1998, 2002, and Spain in 2006, demonstrates the strength of international basketball.

Basketball competitions are held for boys and girls of various ages all around the world. The nationalities represented in the NBA are a reflection of the sport's widespread appeal. The NBA currently has players from each of the six continents with populations. Prominent international athletes started entering the NBA in the mid-1990s, including German Detlef Schrempf, Serbian Vlade Divac, Croatians Draen Petrovic, Toni Kuko, and Lithuanians Arvydas Sabonis, and Arnas Mariulionis.

On April 9, 1975, the Araneta Coliseum in Cubao, Quezon City, hosted the inaugural game of the Philippine Basketball Association. Some teams from the now-dead Manila Industrial and Commercial Athletic Association, which was strictly governed by the Basketball Association of the Philippines (now defunct), the country's then-FIBA-recognized national association, organized it as a "rebellion" and created it. The MICAA fielded nine clubs in the league's inaugural campaign, which got underway on April 9, 1975. The NBL is the top men's professional basketball competition in Australia. The league started in 1979 and played a winter season (April to September) until the 20th season was over in 1998. The first season following the change to the current summer season structure was the 1998–99 season, which started just a few months later (October–April). This change was made to stay out of direct competition with Australia's multiple football codes. Eight Australian teams are participating, along with one from New Zealand. Some athletes, notably Luc Longley, Andrew Gaze, Shane Heal, Chris Anstey, and Andrew Bogut, achieved international success and rose to the status of sports icons in their own Australia. In 1981, the Women's National Basketball League debuted.

Women's Basketball

The first interinstitutional game for women was played in 1891 between the University of California and Miss Head's School. At Smith College, a physical education teacher named Senda Berenson adapted Naismith's rules for female players in 1892, launching the sport of women's basketball. She visited Naismith shortly after being hired by Smith to learn more about the game. She organized the first women's collegiate basketball game on March 21, 1893, pitting her Smith freshmen and sophomores against one another. She was fascinated by the new sport and the moral lessons it could impart. On March 21, 1893, Smith College hosted the first women's intercollegiate basketball game, in which Berenson's freshmen took on the sophomore class. Women started playing basketball at Mount Holyoke and Sophie Newcomb College that same year, both of which were coached by Clara Gregory Baer. By 1895, Wellesley, Vassar, and Bryn Mawr were among the colleges that had adopted the game. On April 4, 1896, the first intercollegiate women's game took place. 9-on-9 action between Stanford women and Berkeley resulted in a 2-1 Stanford victory.

In the beginning, women's basketball growth was more organized than that of males. The American Physical Education Association established the Executive Committee on BasketBall Regulations (National Women's Basketball Committee) in 1905. There were to be six to nine players on each team, and there were to be 11 officials. A women's basketball competition was featured in the International Women's Sports Federation (1924). By 1925, 37 women's High school varsity basketball games or state competitions had taken place. And the first national women's basketball competition, complete with men's rules, was supported by the Amateur Athletic Union in 1926. Between 1915 and 1940, the Edmonton Grads, a traveling Canadian women's team headquartered in Edmonton, Alberta, played. The Grads had a very successful tour across all of North America. At that time, they faced off against any team that wished to fight them, and gate receipts were used to pay for their tours. They amassed a record of 522 victories and just 20 losses. The Grads also excelled during some exhibition trips to Europe and won four straight exhibition Olympic competitions in 1924, 1928, 1932, and 1936. Women's basketball, however, was not recognized as an Olympic sport until 1976. The Grads' players were unpaid and required to maintain their single status. The Grads played with an emphasis on teamwork rather than overemphasizing individual player talent. In 1929, the first female AAU All-America team was selected. All around the country, women's industrial leagues grew up, producing well-known athletes like Babe Didrikson of the Golden Cyclones and the

All-American Red Heads Team, who played against men's teams under men's rules. By 1938, the two-court, six-player women's national championship had replaced the previous three-court format.

The WNBA, which is sponsored by the NBA, was founded in 1997. Although having erratic attendance numbers, the league's popularity and level of competition have benefited from some high-profile players, including Lisa Leslie, Diana Taurasi, and Candace Parker. The popularity of the WNBA has contributed to the demise of several professional women's basketball organizations in the United States, including the American Basketball Association (1996–1998). Several people have viewed the WNBA as a niche league. The league has, however, recently made progress. A deal renewal with ESPN was negotiated by the WNBA in June 2007. The new TV agreement is in effect from 2009 until 2016. The first-ever rights payments to be paid to a women's professional sports league were included in this agreement. "Millions and millions of dollars" will be "dispersed to the league's teams" throughout the contract's eight years. Major League Soccer (253,000) and the NHL both draw fewer viewers (413,000) than the WNBA on national television broadcasts (310,732). NBA Commissioner David Stern stated in a March 12, 2009 article that in a terrible economy, "Compared to the WNBA, the NBA is much less profitable. Between a lot of teams, we're losing a lot of money.

Basketball remains among the most popular sports in the world today.

Basketball is one of the most watched sports in the world, and for good reason. It has a history spanning more than a century. Basketball was developed as an indoor sport, the game immediately became well-known in the US and other nations. After the NBA was founded in 1946, basketball quickly expanded to become a multi-billion dollar enterprise.

The sport quickly gained popularity outside of the US and was ranked among the top sports in almost every country. There are several reasons why basketball is one of the most popular sports.

- Basketball is readily accessible and well-known throughout the world. One of the sports that are currently easy to play is basketball. Almost any location on the planet has a basketball court. This sport can be played and watched live in person, on TV, or online using a streaming platform. The NBA and NCAA are only two of the numerous major leagues that are present both abroad and in the US.

- Together with playing and watching basketball, people also place bets on their favorite teams. Betting on college basketball as well as other major leagues and international events is a typical approach to getting interested in basketball and watching many games each day (Eurobasket, Fiba World Cup, etc.). Basketball fans may now place bets online and watch the games on a desktop or mobile device.

- The best part is, thanks to the power of online streaming platforms, fans from all over the world may now watch all of the main competitions stated above. Over the past 10 years, this has led to an upsurge in the game's popularity.

- Basketball is an easy sport to learn and encourages teamwork. The popularity of basketball is also due to how easy it is to learn. Both amateur and professional basketball players can participate in a variety of simple drills and mini-games, and the rules are very simple. So, this game is fantastic for casual gamers even though millions of players hope to advance their talents and challenge basketball legends like LeBron James.

- Basketball is a group sport that promotes cooperation and strengthens our social skills. Naturally, this also applies to other sports, including rugby and football.

- Basketball is entertaining all around. Finally, basketball is a game that is ultimately entertaining. Basketball is a game that all ages enjoy playing and watching. Particularly when it comes to playing the game, you have the opportunity to have fun while burning calories, improving endurance, improving balance, and more.

The aforementioned makes it very evident that basketball is among the most popular sports for a reason. According to an NBC study, NBA televised games are becoming more and more well-liked around the world. As a result, the popularity of the game is growing every year. The moment is now if you've been thinking about playing or watching basketball.

CHAPTER TWO
Equipment and playing field

The Basketball game is played on a special court with a special set of tools that are intended to promote brisk, high-scoring action. To provide readers with a better knowledge of the key components that enable the game of basketball, this article will examine the tools and court in great depth. Understanding the basketball court and equipment is essential for the success and enjoyment of the game, regardless of your level of experience.

Basketball (ball)

A basketball is a name for the spherical ball used in basketball games. Basketballs frequently come in a range of sizes, from little promotional items with diameters of just a few inches (or centimeters) to extra-large balls with diameters of around two feet (or 60 cm), which are employed in training drills. For example, a child's basketball has a circumference of up to 27 inches (69 cm), whereas the men's and women's basketballs of the National Collegiate Athletic Association (NCAA) have maximum circumferences of 30 inches (76 cm) and 29 inches, respectively (74 cm). The Women's National Basketball Association (WNBA) has a maximum circumference of 29 inches and the National Basketball Association (NBA) has a standard basketball circumference of 29.5 inches (75 cm) (74 cm). High school and junior leagues often use NCAA, NBA, or WNBA-sized balls.

The basketball in play
The ball must be continuously dribbled, passed to other players in the air, or launched toward the basket while playing the game (shooting). The ball must be extremely sturdy and secure. The ball can also be used to perform tricks (also known as freestyling), the most popular of which include spinning the ball on the tip of one's index finger, dribbling in intricate patterns, rolling the ball over one's shoulder, and performing aerobatic maneuvers with the ball while executing a slam dunk, most notably in the context of a slam dunk competition.

Characteristics of a basketball

The inflating inner rubber bladder of a basketball, which is nearly always wrapped with fiber layers before being covered in either leather (the original material), rubber, or a synthetic composite, is a common feature. Like most inflated balls, there is a small aperture that allows the pressure to be adjusted.

The ball's surface is almost always divided into portions by "ribs" that are sunken below the surface in a variety of patterns and are usually a different color. Basketballs can be bought in several colors, but they typically feature an orange surface with black ribs and a possible logo. The Harlem Globetrotters, the American Basketball Association, and the NBA All-Star Weekend Three-Point Contest all used the most well-known variation of these balls, a red, white, and blue ball, as well as it serving as the "money ball" in those competitions.

Depending on whether they are designed for indoor or all-surface use, balls are often made of rubber or durable composites, also known as indoor/outdoor balls, or leather or absorbent composites. Indoor balls are often more expensive than all-surface balls since the materials are more pricey. To get the best grip, new all-leather indoor balls must also be "broken in" before use in competition. Recreational players are advised to utilize an indoor/outdoor ball because an indoor ball is frequently quickly destroyed outdoors due to the abrasiveness of asphalt and the abundance of dirt and wetness. Outdoor balls are usually composed of rubber to survive rougher terrain, and they require more air to maintain reasonable air pressure in colder areas.

History of basketballs

A soccer ball and two peach baskets affixed at the ends of the gym were used for the first basketball game. Basketballs made exclusively for basketball were first made from leather strips stitched together with a rubber bladder within. A textile liner was applied to the leather to boost its consistency and longevity. A replica of the original basketball was created in 1942. The NBA, whose game balls are still made of genuine leather, is the only league that still uses basketball covers made of leather.

After being launched in the late 1990s, synthetic composite materials were swiftly embraced by the majority of leagues (outside of a brief experiment with a microfiber composite ball in 2006 that was not well received). From 1967 until 1976, the American Basketball Association (ABA) adopted a distinctive red, white, and blue basketball. It is employed in the NBA's three-point contest.

Court dimensions and markings

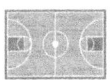

The basketball court is a rectangular playing area with defined dimensions and markings for all levels of play. Although alternative materials, such as asphalt or rubber, can also be used, the court is normally built on a hardwood surface.

The basketball court is one of the biggest playing grounds in sports, measuring 94 feet long and 50 feet wide. There is a basket installed on a 10-foot-high backboard at each end of the court. Four feet separate the basket from the baseline, and four feet separate the sideline from the closest edge of the backboard.

The different parts of the court are distinguished on the playing surface by several lines. The opening tip-off is performed from the center circle, which is situated at the center of the court. For foul shots, the free-throw line is 15 feet away from the basket. To calculate whether a shot is worth two or three points, the three-point line, sometimes referred to as the arc, is employed. It is situated 23 feet 9 inches from the center of the basket.

The half-court line, which splits the court in half and is used to determine which team has possession to start the game and each half, is also indicated on the court. Also used to designate where substitutions can be made during a game are two sets of hash markings that are situated on the sideline.

Generally, the dimensions and markings of the basketball court are intended to ensure fair play and offer players, coaches, and officials clear instructions. For both players and spectators to properly enjoy the action on the court, they must comprehend these markers.

Hoop and net

The net and hoop are two of the most crucial elements in the sport of basketball. The net is fastened to the hoop and hangs down to the base of the basket. The hoop is a circular ring that is mounted to a backboard.

The hoop

The hoop normally has an 18-inch diameter and is composed of steel. The backboard is attached to the hoop by a set of hooks, and its rim is 10 feet above the floor. The rectangular backboard can also be made of acrylic or polycarbonate, but it is commonly constructed of tempered glass.

The net

The net is made up of numerous interlocking loops that hang from the rim of the hoop. Typically, the net is made of a strong, lightweight material like nylon. The net's function is to decelerate the ball as it enters the hoop, making it simpler to view and keep track of the score.

Basketball players must shoot the ball through the hoop and net to score points, hence they are crucial components of the game. Also, the hoop and net have developed into iconic representations of the sport, with fans all around the world being able to recognize them by their distinct appearance and sound.

The hoops and nets used in various basketball competitions come in a wide variety. Some hoops include a rim that can be raised or lowered by the player to meet different playing levels. Others can be transported from one place to another since they are portable.

In conclusion, the net and hoop are crucial elements in basketball. They give players something to shoot toward and provide the thrill and drama of making a point. The hoop and net are essential components of the game and its culture, from the sound of the ball swishing through the net to the sight of a player dunking the ball through the hoop.

Other essential equipment
Aside from the ball, hoop, and net, other pieces of equipment are essential to the game of basketball. These include:

Court Markings:

The basketball court is marked with a variety of lines and markings that define the boundaries of the playing area and indicate the location of various zones and circles. These include the half-court line, the three-point line, the free-throw line, and the key.

Backboard Padding:

To protect players from injury, most basketball hoops are equipped with padding around the backboard. This padding is usually made of foam or another soft material and is designed to absorb the impact of players who come into contact with the backboard.

Scoreboard:

In organized basketball games, a scoreboard is used to keep track of the score, the time remaining in the game, and other important information. Scoreboards can range from simple manual scorekeeping systems to high-tech digital displays that are integrated with other game management systems.

Shot Clock:

In some forms of basketball, such as the professional and collegiate levels, a shot clock is used to limit the amount of time that a team has to shoot the ball. This clock typically counts down from 24 or 30 seconds and helps to keep the game moving at a fast pace.

Jerseys and Shorts:

Basketball players typically wear a uniform consisting of a jersey and shorts. These uniforms are usually made of lightweight, breathable materials that allow for freedom of movement and comfort during the game. The uniforms may also include the player's name and number on the back, as well as the team's logo or colors.

Shoes:

Basketball shoes are specially designed to provide support, traction, and comfort during the game. They typically have high tops to support the ankle and provide stability, as well as specialized sole patterns that are optimized for the movement patterns of basketball players.

In general, these items of gear are necessary for playing basketball and help to ensure that players can do so safely and effectively. Each piece of equipment, from the court markings to the jerseys and shoes, is essential to the game and its culture.

CHAPTER THREE

Number of players, positions in a team, team roster, and game officials

Most people are aware that there are always 10 players on the court in a typical basketball game, with 5 players from each team 'in play' at any given time.

What about the team as a whole, though? How many players will be on the substitute list? Are there any additional team members who are not on the field or on the bench?

League   Maximum Number of Players on team
- FIBA   12
- NBA   15
- WNBA   12
- NCAA   15
- NFHS20

The International Basketball Organization (FIBA) developed traditional basketball regulations to keep things straightforward. There are 12 players on each team, with 5 on the court at any given moment and the remaining players on the bench available for substitution.

The Olympics and the majority of basketball leagues worldwide follow this rule.

NBA:

20 competitors (13 actives, 2 inactive)

One of the most contentious and entertaining sports leagues in the world is the NBA. NBA's incredible dunks and astute assists throughout the previous ten years have made it a must-watch television program. The NBA and NCAA, two American basketball leagues, frequently enact their regulations, which can have an impact on anything from squad size to game duration.

To appreciate the incredible athletic exploits and all-around talent exhibited every single night, it is vital to understand how these players get to the NBA and what defines an NBA roster. As a result, you'll be able to comprehend how they are successful in the league better.

An NBA team may increase its roster by up to 20 players over the offseason. An NBA club can have up to 13 "active" players and two "inactive" players on any one night, although this number lowers to 15 once the season starts.

Because marginal players are given a chance to make the team before the season starts, NBA front offices are permitted to have more players in training camp than on their regular-season roster. Many of these athletes found it difficult to establish long-term residences. Others are foreigners or athletes who have excelled in the NBA's "G-League," which is a developing league.

Two-Way Contract Players; Organizations are permitted to keep two players on their books under two-way contracts in addition to the 15-man "permanent" squad throughout the regular season. Younger players who the front office feels are progressing on the plan are typically handed two-way contracts, allowing them to play for both their NBA organization and G-League affiliate. Furthermore, the compensation of two-way contracts is determined by how many minutes a player logs for each team.

NBA Hardship Exception; The NBA does show flexibility in extraordinary instances, even though the roster size of 15 players is essentially set in stone. A team may be given a hardship exception if they have four or more players who have missed three or more games because of an illness or injury and who are likely to miss more games soon.

This enables them to temporarily boost their roster size to 16 players by adding another member. The NBA has more players than 450, thanks to hardship exemptions, in-season transfers, and two-way players than you would anticipate from 30 clubs with 15 players each.

Deciding Which Players are Active and Inactive; NBA teams are permitted to have up to 13 'active' players available to them on game day, as we've already established. The coaching staff of the squad, which compiles an active roster before tip-off, decides which players will be active or inactive.

The majority of the time, these choices are simple because injuries frequently cause players to miss significant amounts of time from play. Players may also be inactive due to limitations on their participation in the rotation, suspensions, health and safety regulations, or authorized absences from the squad.

Not All Active Players Will Have Minutes on the Court
As a result, active players don't get any playing time and receive a DNP (did not play - coach's decision) in the box score. This is because NBA head coaches normally only rotate between 9 and 10 players during a game. Even if they have access to up to 13 active players, this is still the case.

Of fact, this is a common occurrence in many sports, not just basketball. Several players who are currently in the lineup are there just as backups or to fill out the roster; they aren't expecting to play until something out of the ordinary occurs.

WNBA

12 players

The WNBA adheres to FIBA regulations that place a 12-player maximum for basketball teams. There will always be five members of the same team on the field, and there will be room for up to seven substitutes on the bench.

NCAA

15 players (13 actives, 2 inactive)

The NBA and NCAA both have a similar squad system. During the season, a college basketball team may have up to 15 players. Once more, only 13 "active" players will have the opportunity to step foot on the court during the real game.

High School

20 players

At the high school level, there is a wide range of basketball teams with various numbers of players. Because there are numerous high school leagues and federations in the US, each of which has its own set of rules, this is the case.

Contrarily, the rules of the National Federation of State High School Associations (NFHS) state that varsity and junior varsity teams may not have more than 20 players on their rosters. High school teams may have more players on their rosters than those professional or university teams for two reasons. Schools desire the ability to test out more candidates initially to find young players with promise. Expanding a team makes sense to compensate for high school pupils' lower levels of commitment and higher levels of uncertainty.

Street Basketball
4 (3 players, 1 substitute)
Compared to professional basketball competitions conducted indoors, street basketball often has a less formal organization and less strict enforcement of the rules. Teams of almost any size could participate in a true pickup game.

On a half-court, though, 3-on-3 streetball matches are the norm. This is referred to as 33 basketball, and FIBA has rules for it. This style of basketball is essentially a result of how well-liked street basketball is. In official 3-on-3 basketball games, each team has three players on the court at once and a backup player on hand.

The 5 Basketball Positions in a Team

It's crucial to comprehend the fundamentals of an NBA roster and its current players in addition to the extensive and detailed process that goes into building a roster. As is customary, the following players make up an NBA starting lineup:

- Small Forward,
- Power Forward,
- Center,
- Point Guard,
- Shooting Guard.

Each player plays a crucial part in the overall performance and operation of the team. With these positions come specific obligations and tasks on the court.

For instance, a point guard is typically the team's main ball handler, coordinator, and playmaker. His primary goal is often to keep the squad running smoothly, with getting his teammates involved and scoring as a secondary goal.

The primary duties of a Shooting Guard are shooting and scoring, a Small Forward's goal is typically to produce on both the offensive and defensive ends of the court as the team's best athlete, and a Power Forward is a "big" who also contributes on both ends of the floor, and a Center guards the paint, defends the rim, catches lobs, and is a skilled rebounder.

Although these roles and responsibilities are now interchangeable and flexible due to the great skill sets of today's NBA players, the rudimental nature has mostly persisted.

Striking the Right Balance in a Team Roster
No law specifies the minimum number of players a team must have in any particular position, even though various league office policies make it difficult for front offices to assemble rosters. As a result, teams are free to assemble their rosters however they see fit, with a focus on what the team needs to succeed and compete with its rivals.

For championship-level teams, roster composition will be harmoniously balanced, achieving the ideal ratio of stars, developing young talent, seasoned veterans, and a discernible strategy to solve team flaws. Overall, it's safe to say that assembling a successful NBA team is a difficult endeavor that necessitates a great deal of organization and thought.

Fortunately for us, we can simply enjoy the finished result and recognize the excellence we witness every night across the organization.

It's Not Just The Players
While the number of players on a basketball team has been discussed in terms of the players, let's not forget that there are many others who also significantly contribute to the success of a team.

Of course, the team's overarching strategy is led by the head coach and any assistant coaches. A team doctor is also typically there to safeguard the players' health and security. Dedicated physiotherapists, dietitians, and psychotherapists will be employed by more professional basketball teams to ensure that the players are giving their best effort. Not to be forgotten are the janitor who keeps the court pristine so that the team may practice right away or the devoted basketball fan who always supports his team from the stands. These individuals might all be regarded as teammates on the basketball squad.

The officials in basketball are:-
- The referee (chief referee and two others)
- A timekeeper
- A scorer

- A recorder

Their duties include:-

Chief referee:-
He is the senior official and his duties are:-
- He inspects and approves all equipment
- He tosses the ball at the center to start the play.
- He decides whether a goal shall count in case of disagreement.
- He decides on issues on which the timekeeper and scorer disagree.
- He examines and approves the scores at the end of each half, he also makes decisions on any points not covered by the rules.

Referees:-
The duties of the two referees and combined and include the following:-
- They conduct the game according to the rules.
- They allow a substitute to come onto the court.
- They order time-out and decide whether they become dead.
- They count seconds when a player must play, pass the ball, or be short.

Time-keeper:-
His duties are:-
- To keep an accurate check on the playing time.

- Record both the play time and time for stoppages as provided for in the rule.
- To stop the clock on the following occasions:-

i. At the end of each quarter.
ii. At the end of each half.
iii. When an official signals foul.
iv. Throw-in or violation of the rule.
v. When the 24 seconds signal is sounded.
vi. When an official signals for a time-out.

Scorekeeper:-

His duties are:-
- To take down points scored by each player.
- He records personal and technical fouls of players.
- He signals when the player has a total of five fouls.
- He records the time-out of each team and informs the teams and referees of the number of time-outs each team has had.

Recorder:-

He is responsible for recording the scores of each team on the big board.

CHAPTER FOUR

The objective of the game; Scoring points and Winning the game

To make a goal and score a point are the main goals of basketball.
A goal is scored when the ball enters the hoop or basket. The goal post or hoop for a team is placed in the other team's court.

Basketball has turned into one of the most well-liked sports in the world. Using 13 rules, James Naismith developed the game in 1891 to keep students engaged during the drier months. Both the game and how players score have evolved after over 130 years.

Winning the game
Basketball game outcomes are influenced by a variety of variables, including player skill, teamwork, opponent skill, and even luck. Players need to be able to score points and limit their opponents' chances to score to win a basketball game. An effective plan that considers the advantages and disadvantages of the opposition is also necessary for a team.

A team must also possess the mental toughness to maintain its composure and drive throughout the entire game. A basketball team can position itself to win a game by combining individual skill, team planning, and mental toughness. The winning side in a basketball match is the one with the most points after the contest.

When regulation time expires with a tie, the game is decided over overtime. The winning team in overtime is determined by which side scores first.

Rules of the game
If you are new to basketball, terms like goaltending, backcourt violation, or shot clock could be confusing to you.

The Basics
A court, two teams, two baskets, and a ball - that's all you need.

Players
In basketball, there are ten players on the court at once, five on each team. A team can also have an endless number of replacements with its seven substitute players.

A center, two forwards, and two guards often make up the starting lineup, also known as the starting five. There is also room for variations.

Scoring

Basketball is played using a ball that must be thrown into a basket that is situated 10 feet (3.05 meters) above the surface on each end of the rectangular court. A field goal scores two points, whereas free throws only earn one. When made from beyond the three-point line, the shot is worth three points. After the game's conclusion, the team with the most points wins.

Game length

A game is broken into four 10-minute quarters according to FIBA regulations. Each quarter in the NBA lasts 12 minutes. Five-minute overtime periods are played if there is a tie at the end of regulation to decide the victor.

So, how does scoring work in basketball?

Basketball scoring is accomplished by players shooting the ball from a variety of distances and having the ball land in the basket. One point is awarded for each successful free throw, two points are awarded for shots inside the three-point line, and three points are awarded for shots outside the three-point line. These points can be attained in a variety of ways, so we'll go over each one in more detail below.

How Do Free Throws Work in Basketball?

The one-point play will be the subject of our first analysis. The only option to get one point is to make a free throw, which is available 15 feet from the rim.

One-point play

Free throws are meant to be the simplest way to score a point, as their name suggests, but they are also one of the most underutilized. After a shooting foul occurs, a player is given free throws. For the player to be sent to the free throw line after being fouled, they had to be in the shooting motion. By compensating the player who was fouled, the free throw system is an efficient technique to reduce the number of fouls that occur throughout the course of the game.

The referee will whistle the play dead after a shooting foul and move the player to the free-throw line. The other players on the court will all line up either behind the free throw shooter or underneath the basket, allowing him or her to relax before attempting the shot. Until the shot is up, the other players must remain still.

The shooter will either receive one, two, or three free throw attempts, each of which is worth one point. The method for determining this is as follows:

- The shooter gets one shot if they make the shot while being fouled.

- The shooter gets two chances to make the shot if they foul within the three-point line and miss.

- The shooter gets three chances to make the shot if they foul out beyond the three-point line and miss.

Free throws are intended to be the simplest way to score a point, as was previously said. However, a lack of practice has caused many to perform below expectations at the free throw line.

Various Basketball Techniques to Score Two Points
Basketball players can score two points in several different methods, making it the most popular way to do so. Here's a list of the ways a player can score inside the three-point line:

- **Layup** – When a basketball player makes a layup, they dribble the ball into the paint and softly "laid" it into the hoop. The simplest way to score during a game should, in principle, be a wide-open layup.

- **Dunk** – A slam resembles a layup except that the basketball player hangs on to the rim while throwing the ball into the hoop. Bigger players use it as a more aggressive technique to score in the paint to demonstrate their strength and authority. The alley-oop is another well-liked style of dunking.

- **Floater** – In the current era of basketball, the floater shot, which is comparable to a hook shot, has become a crucial shot. It happens when a player dribbles toward the basket but, rather than assaulting it, quickly stops and raises the ball into the air. It is intended to float sufficiently high to avoid being blocked by the defender.

- **Jump shot** Jump shots, sometimes known as "jumpers," are made by a player leaping into the air and shooting the basketball. Although jump shots are more difficult than layups, they are frequently the most frequent way to score in basketball.

There are numerous options for creating space when taking a jump shot. The catch-and-shoot, fadeaway, step-back jump shot, pull-up jump shot, and bank shot are among the highlights of these.

The Three-Point Line in Basketball

The NBA three-point line is well-known to basketball fans today because it has swiftly become one of the most common ways to score. Despite a wide variety of players honing the technique, the three-point shot has become as showy as it is challenging.

Unbelievably, some 90 years after the game was created, in 1979, the three-point line was added to the game of basketball. The NBA's arc is situated 23 feet, 9 inches from the hoop, and the corners are at a distance of 22 feet.

Three points are granted to the shooter when the ball crosses the three-point line. Just two points are given if the shooter walks on the three-point line while making a shot and the ball gets in the basket. A second opportunity at the free throw line will be given if the shooter receives a foul while attempting a three-pointer.

The three-point jump shot will have modifications to open up additional space, just like the two-point jump shot. There is a chance of some difficult shots, particularly near the conclusion of a quarter when the buzzer sounds, even though you'll hardly ever see a player attempt a floater or hook shot from behind the three-point line.

After the quarter, the player would occasionally try a full-court or half-court shot. Despite the increased difficulty, three points will still be awarded for this.

What Is an And-One in Basketball?

And-ones are hard to come by, but they may give a team the boost it needs to go on the offensive. When a player makes a shot and draws a foul at the same moment, it is known as an and-one. An and-one shooting foul, in contrast to most shooting fouls, only grants the shooter one free throw attempt because they already made the basket.

An and-one will do one of two things for you:
- You will get the chance to convert a two-point play into a three-point play as a result.

- You will have the chance to convert a three-point play into a four-point play as a result.

In fact, in contemporary basketball, the only way a player may score four points in a row is on an and-one that takes place on a three-point shot. When they are fouled close to the three-point line, athletes frequently attempt to make a shot even when they are not prepared to do so. Even if they miss the shot, they still have a chance to make a free throw and salvage something.

CHAPTER FIVE

Fouls in the basketball game

what is a foul in basketball?
Any action against the offensive or defense that involves needless contact is considered a foul. Every foul results in a penalty, although the severity of the penalty depends on the type of infraction. Defensive or offensive fouls are divided into personal, team, technical, and flagrant categories.

A referee will call dozens of fouls during a game. To prevent yourself from committing fouls, it's crucial to comprehend the rules as much as you can because they come rapidly and frequently.

What Is a Personal Foul in Basketball?
A personal foul is committed against a particular player, and it is the first kind of foul. A player commits a foul when they make improper physical contact with another player, as was already explained. Hence, the player who committed the foul receives a personal foul.

Basketball players only get six personal fouls in the NBA before being ejected from the contest, otherwise known as "fouling out," so getting one is a major thing. It takes five fouls in college. As the game progresses, each foul assumes greater significance than its predecessor.

Only during the game in which they were committed do personal fouls count. Each personal foul is tallied as a statistic after the game. While these fouls do not carry over to a player's subsequent game, they do not reset until the game is over.

It's common knowledge that players should expect at least three personals calls per game. It doesn't mean that you will always be called for three, but there is a significant likelihood that you will experience all three of these situations. They are:

- Receiving a foul that is undoubtedly a poor decision, but there is nothing you can do to appeal the decision.

- being fined for making improper contact (charge or a block).

- Getting a foul on purpose with a strategic goal.

Before the game even begins, it's a good idea to chalk yourself up for a combination of these three fouls. Because you are more cautious with the ball and won't take risks until they are worthwhile, it helps you reconsider how you approach the rest of the game.

Of course, there will always be situations in which you must use force. For this reason, striking a balance is crucial. You won't put yourself in a difficult situation when you need to strategically foul down the stretch if you only foul when you have to and only foul when it makes sense.

What Is a Team Foul in Basketball?
It's time to discover what a team foul is now that we are familiar with the definition of a personal foul. Despite how similar they are to one another, the two serve very different functions throughout a basketball game and should be treated as such.

Because all team fouls are personal fouls, there is a lot of confusion when the differences between the two are discussed. However, not all personal fouls are team fouls, and they also don't all adhere to the same regulations. I'll explain.

A personal foul committed by the defense is referred to as a team foul. It is for this reason that defensive fouls are so abhorrent because they affect both the individual player and the team. Offense-related personal fouls are known as just that: personal fouls.

Each team is only allowed five team fouls before being penalized, the same as how each player is only allowed six personal fouls before being ejected. Any personal foul, whether offensive or defensive after a team commits its fourth team foul results in free throws for the fouled player, known as being in the "bonus."

When a team's opponent accumulates ten team fouls in one half during a game of college basketball, they go one step further and give that team a double bonus. In contrast, the college bonus provides the team a 1-and-1 opportunity, meaning that they can only attempt a second free throw if the first one is made. If they miss their first attempt, the ball is in play. But, the additional benefit occurs when the player who was fouled is still awarded two free throws (in college).

In conclusion, personal fouls on defense are seen as a "double whammy" because they raise both your personal and your team's collective foul totals. Keep in mind that collegiate basketball only uses halves. In light of this, college team fouls are reset every half whereas NBA fouls are reset every quarter. Avoid those fouls, both offensive and defensive, to maintain your team and yourself in a winning position.

What Is a Shooting Foul in Basketball?

When a defensive personal foul, often referred to as a team foul, is made while the player is shooting, it is referred to as a shooting foul. Whether or not the team is currently in a bonus, shooting fouls always results in free throws for the player who was fouled. The player who was fouled is given two free throws to make up for the two points they would have been eligible for but for the foul when a shooting foul occurs within the three-point line (either on a shot, layup, floater, or dunk).

In a similar vein, a shooting foul committed outside the three-point line results in three foul shots. The basket counts as long as it occurred in the same motion as the foul if the shooter makes the shot as they are fouled. The shooter receives one free throw as compensation for the foul and a chance at a three-point or four-point play. It's known as an and-one.

Recently, the NBA changed a rule that requires the defender to give a shooter enough space to land after shooting. If the defender makes any contact with an opponent while they're still in the air, it's likely to be called a foul. The new rule has caused the four-point play to become much more common than it used to be.

What Is a Technical Foul in Basketball?

One of the worst penalties in a basketball game is a technical foul, sometimes known as a "T" or "tech". If a player is acting out of control, it may be handed to them on the field, on the bench, or even to the coach. A technical foul typically results from unsportsmanlike behavior. Each technical foul often belongs to one of six categories, which are further described below.

- **Excessive Timeouts**– A technical foul is called against the coach who requests a timeout when there are none left. The other team is given a free throw, and the team that makes the free shot is the one who gets the ball next.

- **Delay of Game** – any unnecessary action that results in the game being delayed, such as a player preventing another player from inbounding the ball, ends in a technical foul being assessed. Even actions that result in a one-second delay can be called a technical foul.

- **Number of Players**- Any team that has six or more players on the court is in violation. When this occurs, a technical foul is signaled.

- **Basketball Rim** –
  It is a technical foul to use the rim or backboard to your advantage to maintain balance or jump higher. The basketball net cannot be purposefully hung on for an extended amount of time by players.

- **Conduct** – much like any sport, players need to know how to carry themselves and how to properly represent the NBA and the rest of their team. Any unsportsmanlike conduct is bound to be given a technical foul, if not a warning.

- **Fighting** – On the basketball court, fighting is prohibited in addition to unsportsmanlike behavior. This involves conflicts between athletes, coaches, or officials that are verbal or physical.

It is ultimately up to the referee to determine whether a technical foul should be called given the variety of possible circumstances. The referee may issue a warning before issuing a technical foul for the majority of the rules mentioned above. The opposite side usually receives a free throw and possession of the ball when a technical foul is called. The sanctions increase as you rack up technical fouls throughout the season.

Once enough technical fouls are accrued, a suspension might eventually be imposed. In the playoffs, fines are even worse. Receiving two technicals in the same game results in dismissal from that game, whether you're a player or a coach. It doesn't matter how serious those fouls are as long as they both result in technical fouls.

What Is a Flagrant Foul in Basketball?
Flagrant fouls are the most aggressive type of foul there is. Although they aren't called as frequently as other infractions, they undoubtedly stir up feelings when they are. Flagrant fouls are thought to be over the top, pointless, or malicious. It's usually a difficult decision for the referee to make, and typically a video review is needed to determine the reason for the illegal contact.

The referee must decide whether a foul is a "Flagrant Foul 1" or a "Flagrant Foul 2" even though it is a flagrant foul. That is a difficult call for the referee because the difference between the two can alter the outcome of a game. When a foul is deemed unnecessary but not excessively so, it is classified as a flagrant foul 1. When the violation is found to be both unnecessary and excessive, it is classified as a flagrant foul 2. A flagrant foul 1 that is committed twice will result in ejection, while a flagrant foul 2 that is committed only once will result in ejection.

Flagrant fouls also result in ejections, which is a major plus, but they also give the opposing team free throws and possession of the ball. Depending on how egregious the foul is, players who commit it typically face a fine or suspension.

Offensive Fouls in Basketball
Offensive fouls are, as the name implies, fouls committed on the offense. They are typically called when an illegal obstruction prevents the defense from taking the necessary action. There will always be some sort of physical interaction.

Here are the top five offensive fouls that have been called in the NBA:

Charging – When an attacking player collides with a defender who is standing stationary with his feet planted, it is deemed a foul. The defensive player typically retreats to sell the call.

Illegal Screen – The referee declares a screen by an attacking player to be unlawful if it is set while the player is in motion.

Holding – Both the offense and the defense are called for this infraction. It happens when a player purposefully holds another player to eliminate their range of motion.

Elbowing – A personal foul is signaled by the referee whenever a player elbows another player. The offense is prone to get called for elbowing when making space for themselves or driving to the basket, even though it occurs on both sides of the ball.

Over the Back – This infraction is typically noted when attempting to grab an offensive rebound. It occurs when a player grabs a rebound by reaching behind the defender.

Although they don't happen as frequently as defensive fouls, offensive fouls are just as tragic. When you make an offensive foul, you lose control of the ball and your chance to score. If the opposition team is in the bonus, which gives them possession of the ball for free throws, the penalty is significantly harsher.

Play your game, not the one your defender wants you to play if you want to avoid an offensive penalty. Keep your attention on the play and your duties in the foreground. By doing that, on the defensive play.you compel the defense to move and increase the likelihood of committing a foul.

Defensive Fouls in Basketball
These are fouls committed while on defensive play. Some defensive fouls;

Hand Check – This offense, sometimes known as "illegal use of hands," is committed when a defensive player makes illegal contact with an opponent while using their hands. Due to the constant back-and-forth between players, it's typically a difficult call for the referee to make.

Reaching In – while the defense wants to try and steal the ball from the offense, they can't force it by making contact with the offensive player. If they get 'all-ball', then the referee won't call it a foul.

Tripping – This is a foul in almost every sport and is considered unneeded by all. Both the offense and the defense can call it, although it usually happens when there is a lost ball.

Blocking Foul – This infraction is frequently signaled when a defender tries to force a charge. It takes time for the defense to set up before it can make contact with an offensive player. They are not set, so it is a foul.

Pushing Although tight defense is typically taught to the defenders, it occasionally backfires. Basketball games move so quickly that playing tight defense might occasionally lead to a push. Since defensive fouls also count towards the team foul count, it's best to avoid these types of fouls as much as possible. There are times when a defensive foul is needed, especially late in the game when you want to stop the clock.

Knowing when to foul is a skill not many players have these days. Instead, the NBA today sees a lot of players deliberately trying to get fouled and flopping on the floor. Unfortunately, this takes away from the game of basketball and referees don't allow it — so much so that excessive flopping is a foul in itself.

What Is a Free Throw in Basketball?
For any offensive player, the free throw, often known as the "foul shot" and the "charity stripe," is their closest friend. The attacking player has complete control over just one play throughout the whole basketball game. Every player should be proficient at this one shot, too.

Any offensive player who commits a shooting foul will receive free throws. Free throws are supposed to restore their chance to score if they are fouled while taking a shot. When in the bonus, the defense receives compensation as well.

Four hashes are visible on each side of the rectangle when you look at the painted area. The players' positions when lining up for a free throw are shown by the hashes. Up until the ball leaves the shooter's hand, they must stay outside the paint area.

A 15-foot distance separates the basket from the actual free-throw line. Although they can shoot from a 12-foot-wide line, players typically opt to do it in the center of the area. Also, players have ten seconds to make a shot before giving it up.

The number of free throws you receive is either one, two, or three. If the shooter is fouled while draining a three-pointer, a free throw can result in a maximum four-point play.

Aim for a free throw percentage of no less than 80% because the defenders won't be putting up any fight when you attempt one. Sometimes the person who is going to make the free throw is the only one on the hashes, so they can make the shot. This is typical of a technical foul.

CHAPTER SIX

Violations in Basketball and Time Regulations

Contrary to common opinion, fouls and violations are not interchangeable terms. Regrettably, a lot of people confuse things by combining fouls and violations.

A foul typically entails impermissible physical contact between two players, as we previously mentioned. On the other side, a violation entails using the ball or court in an unsportsmanlike manner.

For example, the following are considered violations in basketball — as opposed to fouls:

Double-Dribble-
When a player dribbles with both hands simultaneously or continues to dribble after letting the ball rest in either one or both hands.

Traveling-;
when a player improperly establishes the pivot foot or illegally moves their pivot foot.

Palming;
When a player isn't dribbling with their hand on top of the ball, it's known as a carry or a carry.

Held-Ball violation;
When two players fight for the ball and neither player is giving way, it's called a held ball or 'jump ball'.

Backcourt;
The team cannot move the ball into the backcourt when a player dribbles past half-court until the ball is changed hands.

Kicking;
The referee stops play whenever a player kicks the ball, whether intentionally or unintentionally.

Out-of-bounds;
The ball is considered to be out of bounds if it or the player carrying it contacts the ground along or behind the sideline.

Free Throw Violation;
A free throw is invalidated if the offensive team enters the paint area while shooting it. The offense is given another opportunity to attempt the free throw if the defensive player enters the paint while the opposing team is shooting.

Infraction of the three-second rule;
When on offense, players are not allowed to remain in the key for longer than three seconds.

Violation of the 5-Second rule;
Each attacking player gets five seconds to act with the ball when being tightly guarded. Players have five seconds to inbound the ball before a play.

The eight-second rule;
Players have eight seconds after the ball is inbounded to advance it past half-court without breaking the eight-second rule.

24-second rule violation:
The offender has 24 seconds to get a shot off. The shot clock resets to 14 seconds if they recover the ball after it hits the rim.

Goaltending;
Goaltending occurs when a defensive player stops the ball from entering the basket after it has already begun to fall, giving the offense the necessary points.

Although most violations happen on offense and result in a change in ball possession, some violations happen on defense as well. One of the key distinctions between fouls and violations is that no free throws will be given for a violation.

What is a Carry in Basketball?

Because of the action the player takes when they violate the rule, it is known as a "carry" rule. Instead of dribbling the basketball, it appears as though they are "carrying" it with their hand. The NBA's definition of a carrying violation is as follows:

"A player who is dribbling may not place any portion of his hand under the ball and (1) carry it from point to point or (2) bring it to a stop and then resume dribbling."

Players must dribble with their hands on top of the basketball, as required by the rule. It is a carry when their hand passes underneath and they continue to dribble after that. The rule also prohibits players from holding the ball while pausing to dribble before continuing.

This should not be confused with a double dribble, which is when a player dribbles, fully pick up the ball and then resumes dribbling. If there is only a "pause" in the dribble while it is still in one hand, followed by a continuation, it is referred to as a "carrying violation".

Why is Carrying a Basketball Illegal?
Dribbling is a key fundamental of basketball. Players pick up new dribbling techniques as they advance to evade defenders. Carrying, however, would give the player a substantial edge if it were permitted. The dribbler could have an undue advantage.

The defense has a better chance of stopping the basketball if players are forced to keep their hands on top of the ball while dribbling. It would be extremely difficult to play effective defense if the offense could carry the ball rather than maintain their dribble.

What's the Penalty for Carrying?
The same as a double dribble or travel, a carry results in a dead-ball turnover. The sideline or baseline that is closest to the location of the violation is used to toss the ball in high school and college. In the NBA, however, the ball is inbounded between the free throw line and baseline to give the defense an edge.

Should Carrying Get Called More Often?
Critics frequently claim that infractions like carrying and traveling aren't called out sufficiently. NBA players are experts at what they do. To become the best basketball players in the world, they put in countless hours of practice. What most people assume to be a carry is frequently not.

NBA players frequently "pocket dribble," which involves having their hand behind the ball but not underneath it. This pocket dribble is sometimes referred to as a hesitation move. To the untrained eye, it might appear to be a carry, but it isn't. The wait isn't long enough to qualify as a violation, as the ball never goes beneath the player's hand.

Referees are extremely trained to recognize the variances and blow their whistle when a legitimate carry occurs, especially in the NBA. In juvenile basketball, carrying calls occur most frequently. The fundamentals of the game, including effective dribbling tactics, are still being learned by young players.

Ways you may see carrying called in a youth basketball game include:
- The player is dribbling too high and the hand is placed underneath the ball.

- Player hesitates with their dribble, and their hand slides under the ball.

- The player is sprinting while trying to control their dribble, leading to a carry.

- The player is stationary dribbling and accidentally palms the basketball.

If players frequently carry the basketball, it's incredibly important their coach corrects it. If players aren't taught proper dribbling, their poor habits will be extremely hard to break.

What's the best way to do it?
Small-sided games are another excellent approach to training players to avoid carrying the ball. Also, stationary ball-handling drills and cone drills have their place in training.

Players can hone their dribbling techniques by playing small-sided games. Players can apply the skills they develop in stationary and cone drills in a genuine competition because these exercises simulate the situations they'll face in a live game.

Conclusion
When a player is dribbling and their hand touches the basketball, it is ruled that they are carrying the ball. Youth settings frequently use it more than high school, college, or professional games do.

Teams who can minimize carrying will have more possessions and hence more scoring opportunities. Players can prevent carrying and turning the ball over with practice and the right instruction.

Time regulations
How long is a basketball game?
There is a predetermined time limit for basketball games. With various leagues and playing levels, it varies:

- Four 8-minute quarters or two 16-minute halves are used in high school basketball games.

- Two 20-minute halves make up an NCAA college basketball game. This holds for both international and WNBA competitions.

- Four 12-minute quarters comprise an NBA game.

How long does the timer last?
- When the ball is in play, the clock starts to tick.
- When the ball is out of bounds, a foul is called, a free throw is made, or a timeout is used, and the clock is paused.
- The clock begins when a player touches the ball during an inbound play.
- During the final two minutes of regulation time and overtime in the NBA, the clock stops when a shot is made.
- During college games, overtime and the final minute of the contest are stopped.

Overtime

If there is a draw at the end of regulation, overtime will be played. Most leagues limit overtime to 5 minutes. There will be more overtime added till one team wins.

The Shot Clock

A shot clock was added to the game to speed it up and stop teams from stalling. You have this amount of time to shoot the ball. The shot clock resets if the ball changes hands or touches the basket rim. Several basketball leagues have different shot clock lengths:

- Collegiate men in the NCAA - 35 seconds

- Collegiate women in the NCAA - 30 seconds

- 24 seconds in the NBA

There isn't a shot clock for high school in every state. Where they do, it usually complies with NCAA regulations.

Time outs

Teams can use time outs to rest their players, call plays, or just halt play for a bit. Several leagues have various time-out policies:

High school: The coach or players on the court have the authority to request a timeout. Each game has five timeouts, three of which are 60 seconds long and two of which are 30 seconds long.

NCAA College - The number of timeouts varies depending on whether the game is shown on television or not. This is so that commercial breaks can be used by the TV broadcaster to air advertisements during TV games. Each side is allotted one 60-second timeout and four 30-second timeouts for a television game. Each team has four 75-second and two 30-second time-outs during a non-televised game.

NBA - Each basketball team in the NBA is allowed six full timeouts and one 20-second timeout per half. A time-out can only be requested by one player at a time.

CHAPTER SEVEN
Dribbling the Basketball

Dribbling

There are two ways to move the basketball. The preferred and quicker method is the pass. However, if the defense is tight and the passing lanes are clogged, the dribble is used to set up the offense. Since the dribble can only begin and stop one time it is in a player's possession, he should make his dribble count. It has to have a purpose. The dribble, along with the pass and the shot is one of the offensive triple threats every player must have in his arsenal. Use the dribble to:

- Move the ball on offense.

- Blow past your man to the hoop.

- Escape from a tough and sticky defense.

- Shoot.

- Move around a screen and get off your shot behind it.

- Get a better passing angle.

- Freeze the ball in the closing minutes.

Don't pound the air out of the ball going nowhere. If you want to get from point "A" to point "B", do it with the least amount of dribbling that's possible. Once you put the ball on the floor, it should be to help you get where you want to go. If the dribble can't help you, pass it to a teammate.

How to Dribble

Contrary to popular belief, dribbling is not performed while gazing at the ball, as many young players do. Without looking at the ball, you dribble with your fingers and hand pads. Always keep your head up. Keep your gaze fixed on the action taking place on the court. A basketball with the right air pressure will always rebound straight up at least 75% of the height it was dropped from. As a result, you can dribble without having to look at the ball. Use your fingertips to "see". Simply said, the ball can be felt and controlled by those fingers. Push the ball down when dribbling by spreading your fingers and flexing your wrist. It doesn't need to be pushed down firmly. Simple pressure is sufficient. Also, maintain a straight back and flexed legs so that you are prepared to act quickly. Every player should become proficient at dribbling with both hands. Your offensive options will increase thanks to this ambidextrous trait. The defender will be deterred from trying to overplay your strong side. Every time you choose to place the ball on the floor, there is one crucial principle to bear in mind. Before starting your dribble, decide what you're going to do with the ball.

Types of Dribbles:

There are about as many types of dribbles as there are players. The important ones will be discussed in this chapter. If you want to be a good player, practice enough that you can use them whenever a situation arises.

The Low Dribble;

Anytime you are being closely guarded, you should use the low dribble. Just keeping the ball under control and low to the ground constitutes this kind of dribbling. To minimize the distance the ball must travel, extend your dribbling hand and arm as far down as you can. Your dribbling hand's elbow should remain close to your side. On your body's side, dribble the ball away from the defender. You maintain your dribbling hand's palm over the ball at all times. As you dribble, don't look at the ball. Examine the court and consider your alternatives. The ball can be protected from the defender by using your other forearm. Avoid pushing or shoving the defender with your forearm when being closely guarded.

The Speed Dribble;

In the open court, you must move with the ball as swiftly as you can while keeping both the ball and your body under control. Because you are not being tightly guarded in this scenario, maintaining maximum speed is more crucial than protecting the ball from the opposition. To go swiftly and dribble at the same time, push the ball out in front of you at waist height and dash after it. To view your teammates, the full court, and any defenders in front of you, keep your vantage point up. The faster you run, the more the ball needs to be pushed in front of you. This kind of dribble positions your hand behind the ball instead of directly above it, like in the low dribble, to push the ball firmly and in front of you with your arm fully extended (at almost a 45-degree angle to the floor). In order to control the ball as you sprint down the court, the speed dribble asks for a high bounce, but be careful that it doesn't reach higher than hip level.

The Change-Of-Pace Dribble;

One of the most popular dribbles, it's utilized to fool defenders into thinking you're slowing down or about to pick up your dribble and halt. Slow down your dribble and nearly stop it when your man is closely guarding you. Maintain your dribble while arching your back as though you were searching for a teammate to pass to. As the person guarding you relaxes his defense, suddenly crouch down and dribble the ball far and hard. Burst past him with all your might while keeping the ball in your free hand. The hand dribbling the ball moves from above it to behind it, almost at a 45-degree angle to the ground.

The Crossover Dribble;

The crossover dribble calls for dribbling with one hand, pushing the ball out in front of you with the other hand as you approach your defender, and launching past him. This move can help you lose your defender, but if you don't execute it well, the defense may be able to steal the ball from you as you make the crossover. While you dribble, keep the ball low. While you are close to the defender and dribbling with your right hand, bounce the ball to your left side, close to your left foot. To knock the ball over, the right hand must remain by its side. Hold your left hand poised to catch the ball, holding it perpendicular to the floor for a brief moment to stop its motion before pushing it out in front of you. Remain low and shift your weight by pushing with the inside of your right foot in the new direction. To fend off the defense, lower your right shoulder and use your trunk to hold the ball. Make the closest cut you can to your defender. Combine the crossover dribble with a change of pace for the best outcomes.

The Between-The-Legs Dribble;

When you are being closely guarded or when you are being overplayed and need to shift your dribbling direction, this dribble is a rapid way to transfer the ball from one hand to the other. Consider a scenario in which you are dribbling with your right hand and wish to switch to using your left. Maintain a low dribble. Put your right hand laterally on the ball's outside during the final dribble you make before the changeover and forcefully push it between your open legs. To catch the ball with your left hand's fingers extended wide and pointing downward, you must be close to your legs. Using your left hand, keep dribbling.

The Reverse Dribble;
Another dribble to use when being heavily guarded is this one. The dribbler will momentarily lose sight of his teammates and other defenders while the move is being made, which is a big disadvantage. Stop abruptly for a half-second when you approach the defense. Keep your body low and turn your back on your defender while pivoting with your left foot (assuming you are dribbling right-handed). To execute this, pivot on your left foot while moving your right leg, right shoulder, and head to the left. While you pivot on your left foot, continue to dribble with your right hand. While you turn, keep your feet apart as much as possible to maintain your balance. To help the rest of your body make the turn, the right foot must be quickly turned and pointed in the new direction. Swing your right arm and shoulder to aid in your rotation for swift execution of the maneuver. Pushing the ball from the side and rotating it requires shifting your right hand from the top of the ball to your right side. With your first bounce, slam the ball firmly to the ground. It has to cross your left foot laterally. The left hand is then used to carry on the dribble.

The Half-Reverse Dribble;
Start the move just as you would the normal reverse dribble. Make a 90-degree turn and then come back to your original position. To be effective, the move must be done quickly. Keep your palm on the side of the ball for the first 90-degree turn and then switch it to the other side of the ball when you bring it back to the starting position.

The Hockey Dribble;

The hockey dribble is a staggered dribble maneuver that incorporates a head-and-shoulder fake with a shift in direction and is designed to fool a defender. Stay low and keep the ball by your side to make this move. Do little "stutter" steps (short, fast, parallel steps) with your foot as you approach the defender. Do head-and-shoulder fakes at the same moment to trick the defense. When dribbling with your right hand, pretend to move to the left with your left foot and left shoulder while keeping up your dribble. Next swiftly turn around, accelerate, and with your right hand push the ball out. Your right leg should be leading the way as you get past the defender. You might also want to employ a crossover dribble to go past your defender in specific circumstances.

The Behind-The-Back Dribble;

Change your direction slightly to the left when you get closer to the defender on your right side in order to pass past him. After making your final dribble with your right hand, push the ball to your left side by sliding your palm over and then outside on it, swinging it behind and across your lower back. Your right arm should stop moving as closely as feasible to your left hip. You'll have the most ball control if you do this. As soon as you have the ball in your left hand and are making the first dribble, quicken your pace. The first bounce on the left side must be made well out in front and to the side of the left foot if you want this technique to function particularly well.

The Backup Dribble;

This dribbling move is mostly utilized to get out of a risky defensive scenario. Turn your shoulder toward the defender while dribbling with your right hand. Push back with your left foot while dribbling with your left hand. Your left shoulder and arm should be used to shield the ball.

Ball Handling & Dribble Drills;

It takes a lot of practice holding the ball in your hands before you can master the art of dribbling. The only way to develop your dribbling abilities is to practice, just like you would with any offensive basketball motion. Avoid looking at the ball as much as you can when you are practicing dribbling. Simple exercises for beginners include carrying a basketball with you wherever you go. While you make your way to school or to see a friend, dribble the ball. Take the ball with you the next time you go for a jog and dribble it the entire way. With some practice, you'll find that dribbling the ball comes naturally to you and that you don't even have to think about it. To improve your court skills, practice the specialized dribbling moves (such as the behind-the-back dribble, between-the-legs dribble, etc.) once you have mastered dribbling the ball without looking at it. It's crucial to keep in mind that before attempting to execute the dribble motion at game speed, you must first grasp the actual dribbling mechanics of each move. First, practice them slowly. After getting used to the ball at a slow speed, gradually increase the speed. The drills listed below are easy enough for you to practice on your own.

Around The Legs;

Keep your feet shoulder's width apart. Flex your knees and bend over at your waist. Holding the ball in your right hand, move it between your legs and around your left knee. Pick the ball up with your left hand, swing it around the front of your left knee and back to your right hand. Repeat. Do 20 repetitions of this drill on your left leg and then repeat it on your right leg.

Around The Knees;

Keep your feet a few inches apart, flex your knees, and bend at the waist. Holding the ball in your right hand, pass it behind your knees to your left hand. Pass the ball around the front of your knees with your left hand to your right hand. Repeat the drill 20 times going in one direction as quickly as possible. Change direction and repeat the drill again.

Around The Waist;

Stand up straight with your feet a shoulder's width apart. Hold the ball at waist level in your right hand and pass it behind your back as far as possible to your left hand. Pass the ball around the front of your waist as far as possible to your right hand. Repeat the drill 20 times going as quickly as possible. Change direction and repeat the drill again.

The Figure-8;
Keep your feet spread wider than a shoulder's width, flex your knees, and bend forward at the waist. Holding the ball at knee level in your right hand, pass it behind your left leg to your left hand. Pass it around the front of your left leg to behind your right knee to your right hand. Pass it around the front of your right knee to the back of your left knee. Repeat the drill 15 times going as quickly as possible. Change direction and repeat the drill. Don't watch the ball.

Figure-8 With Drop In The Middle;
This drill is done exactly as the figure-8, except each time that you bring the ball between your legs from the front, drop it. Picking it up on the bounce, continue the drill as before. Repeat the drill 15 times going as quickly as possible. Change direction and repeat the drill. Don't watch the ball.

Between-The-Legs Run; This ball-handling drill is a good prelude to the between-the-legs dribbling drill. Assume a crouched position and begin moving slowly down the court. As you move, pass the ball quickly from your right hand between your legs to the back of your left leg to your left hand. With the left hand, pass the ball around the front of your left leg, between your legs to the back of your right leg to your right hand. Repeat the drill continuously while moving down the court.

Between-The-Legs Bounce;

And Catch Holding the ball over your head with two hands, spread your feet slightly further than shoulder's width. Swing the ball forward and bounce it on the floor between your legs near your heels. Swing your arms back quickly and catch the ball with your two hands as it bounces up toward your hips. Repeat this drill 15 times as quickly as possible.

Ball Drop/Hand;

Here's a tricky drill that

requires quickness and, since you won't be looking at the ball, a sense of where the ball is. Flex your knees, keep your feet together, and bend forward at the waist. Holding the ball behind your knees, let it drop to the floor. Bring your hands to the front of your knees, clap them together, then quickly bring them behind your knees to pick the ball up before the next bounce. Repeat this drill 15 times.

Sit Dribbling;

Legs crossed in front of you, sit down on the floor. Start dribbling the ball around your back as far as you can to your left hip with it in your right hand. As far as you can in front of you, dribble the ball to your right hand while passing it to your left. fifteen times, switch directions and then repeat the exercise.

Full-Court Speed Dribble;

Move quickly down the court with the ball waist-high and far out in front of you. Make the lay-up and head back up court, repeating the speed dribble and lay-up. Do this 6 times. Shoot 10 free throws, then repeat the drill.

Crossover Dribble;

Set up a series of folding chairs on the basketball court about 10 to 15 feet apart. Pretend that they are defensive players trying to grab at the ball. Begin at one end of the court and dribble around the chairs, weaving your way to the end. As you approach each chair, change your dribbling hand, remembering to keep the ball low and close to your body.

Reverse Dribble;

Place three chairs 15 feet apart on the court and pretend that they are defensive players. Dribble toward them and make your spin move, using proper form and technique. When you arrive at the next chair, repeat the move. On your return trip, try to make the move with the other hand. Keep practicing.

CHAPTER EIGHT

Shooting the ball, rules of substitution, and the greatest players

Shooting the ball

The primary skill in basketball is shooting. If you can't put the ball in the basket, you won't score. When you practice shooting, you should practice with good fundamentals. Shooting the correct way will give consistency to your shots and allow you to become an excellent shooter.

Stance and Balance

Balance is crucial when shooting. You should strike the balls of your feet while standing with your feet apart. Jump straight up as you attempt a jump shot. Consistency is much harder if you veer off to the side or in the direction of the hoop. Maintain a straight shoulder line with the basket.

Use Your Legs

Use your legs for strength when you fire. You will start to lose accuracy if you have to utilize all of your arm strength to get the ball through the hoop. Let your arms and hands target and control while using your legs to generate power. This entails jumping as you release the ball while bending your knees. Jumping high when making a jump shot will also prevent your shot from being blocked.

Holding the Ball (Shoot with one hand)
It matters how you hold the ball. The majority of your shots will be made with one hand. Never use two hands to make an outside shot. The only method to consistently maintain your shot straight when shooting is with one hand. Hold the ball in one hand while maintaining balance with the other. Stretch your fingers on the primary shooting hand a little. Hold the ball high, right in front of and just above your head.

That Elbow
The elbow in is maybe the most crucial thing for a young shooter to practice. The ball, your elbow, and your arm should all be parallel to the hoop. This is crucial for maintaining the straightness of your shot. The hoop should be the target of your elbow.

Shooting the Ball
You will now let the ball go. Use your arms to direct the ball and your legs for power, as we discussed previously. the ball upward and in the direction of the goal. Point your elbow, your arms, and your hands toward the basket.pg

Follow Through

Take the shot and finish it. Finally, flick your wrist. Consider "grabbing the rim" when you release the ball as one way to conceptualize this. This will improve touch and keep the ball straight.

A properly executed follow-through will result in some backspin on the ball. Your shot will have "touch" thanks to the backspin. The rim can be touched, allowing the ball to gently rebound. If your shot is slightly off, you have a greater chance of getting the roll and still making the basket as a result.

Get Some Arc on that Shot

An accurate shot should have some arc to it. Arc increases the likelihood that the ball will land in the basket. In essence, it increases the basket's size and provides a better angle. A flat shot has a small angle and a substantially lower probability of finding the hoop.

Practice

Basketball shooting practice is the best approach to improvement. You must practice shooting correctly, though. You'll be able to shoot consistently and form solid habits as a result of this.

Substitutions

The number of player replacements permitted during a basketball game is essentially limitless. Coaches frequently make substitutions to create the best possible matchups against the opposing team, to give players a break when they are worn out, or to remove players from the game who have accumulated too many fouls. Knowing the regulations of basketball governing substitution might assist coaches to avoid penalties.

Notifying Scorer's Table
When a player wishes to take the place of another, they must notify the scorer's table. Before joining the game, the player must present his jersey number to the official scorekeeper and wait at the scorer's table. The scoreboard operator is responsible for blowing the horn to notify the referees that a player intends to substitute into the game. A substitute may not enter the field of play until the referee calls them to do so.

Legal Substitution
Except for during the final minute of play in collegiate games and after a made basket in the National Basketball Association, substitutes are only permitted to join the game when the ball is dead and the clock has stopped (NBA). A technical foul is committed whenever a player enters the game before the authorities have beckoned them to do so.

When this happens in high school, the opposition team receives the ball and is given two free throws as punishment. In college, the other team merely gets two free throws, and then the team that had possession of the ball last before the technical foul was called gets the chance to retake possession. Like in college, the NBA only allows the opposing team to shoot one free throw.

Greatest of players;
Over the history of the NBA, which has spanned nearly 75 years, we have seen a wide range of players display elite scoring talent. There's a reason all the greatest basketball talent in the world comes to the NBA and it's because that's where legends are born.

Taking a look at the top-25 greatest scorers in NBA history, only two of them are still actively pursuing an NBA career — and doing well at that. LeBron James (No. 3 all-time) and Carmelo Anthony (No. 17 all-time) both entered the league in 2003 and have enjoyed some of the greatest careers we've seen in a long time.

Here's a list of the top-25 greatest scorers in NBA history:

- Kareem Abdul-Jabbar
- Karl Malone
- LeBron James

- Kobe Bryant
- Michael Jordan
- Dirk Nowitzki
- Will Chamberlain
- Shaquille O'Neal
- Moses Malone
- Elvin Hayes
- Hakeem Olajuwon
- Oscar Robertson
- Dominique Wilkins
- Tim Duncan
- Paul Pierce
- John Havlicek
- Carmelo Anthony
- Kevin Garnett
- Vince Carter
- Alex English
- Reggie Miller
- Jerry West
- Patrick Ewing
- Ray Allen
- Allen Iverson

When it comes to active players in today's NBA — outside of LeBron James and Carmelo Anthony — there are plenty of scorers that could find themselves on this list very soon. Kevin Durant (22,940 points) and James Harden (20,723 points) are the closest, but Russell Westbrook (20,315 points) and LaMarcus Aldridge (19,599 points) are right behind them.

It will take a ton of practice and unmatched commitment if you hope to one day score as well as these all-time greats. For those who truly desire something, simply keep trying hard and never give up. Don't overlook the process; even the best players constantly strive to get better.

Summary

On a rectangular court, basketball is played by two teams of five players. The goal of the game is to pass the ball through a hoop that is 10 feet above the ground to score points. When the game is over, the team with the most points wins.

As part of the jump ball start to the game, the referee throws the ball up between two players from each team. The team that successfully seizes control of the ball is referred to as the offensive, while the opposition is referred to as the defensive. To put the ball in the hoop, the offensive team gets 24 seconds. Defending team gains possession if they don't.

The game is split into four quarters of 12 minutes each at the professional level. Basketball games in high school and college could have shorter quarters. There is a halftime break following the second quarter.

Once the ball enters the goal, a player scores. In comparison to successful shots beyond the three-point line, successful shots within the three-point line are worth two points instead of three. Free throws are awarded if an opponent fouled a player. The fouled player may attempt one or two free shots, depending on the type of foul. Each made free throw results in a point being awarded.

A set of guidelines for the game of basketball have been produced by the National Basketball Association and the International Basketball Federation (FIBA) (NBA). The number of players who may be on the court at one time as well as the dimensions of the court are all limited by these regulations. They also list the many fouls that can be committed along with the penalties that go along with them.

One of the most essential basketball laws is the 24-second shot clock. Within 24 seconds of recovering control, the offensive team is required to shoot the ball under these rules. Failure to do so results in a turnover, which gives the ball to the opposing team.

It's important to follow the five-foul rule. A player can only commit a total of five personal fouls before being dismissed from the game. A personal foul is deemed to have been committed whenever a player makes illegal contact with one of the opposing team's players.

Basketball games are also governed by a set of guidelines known as the "spirit of the game". These ideals emphasize sportsmanship, fair play, and respect for the opposing team and the referees. These guidelines and the game's fairness must always be upheld by participants.

Conclusion

Basketball is a quick-moving, exhilarating sport that requires skill, planning, and teamwork. Played on a rectangular court, the game consists of two teams of five players each. To score points, the player must put the ball into the hoop. The game's rules and core principles place a strong emphasis on fair play, sportsmanship, and respect for the game and its players. Millions of people worldwide continue to play basketball, making it one of the most well-liked sports now in existence.

Printed in Great Britain
by Amazon